MW00723339

MARILYN MONROE

MARILYN
MONROE

BY JULIE MARS

ARIEL BOOKS

ANDREWS AND McMEEL

KANSAS CITY

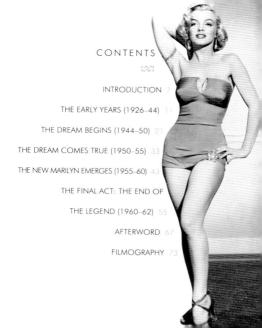

CONTENTS

INTRODUCTION 7

THE EARLY YEARS (1926–44) 11

THE DREAM BEGINS (1944–50) 21

THE DREAM COMES TRUE (1950–55) 33

THE NEW MARILYN EMERGES (1955–60) 43

THE FINAL ACT: THE END OF

THE LEGEND (1960–62) 55

AFTERWORD 67

FILMOGRAPHY 73

EARLY ON AUGUST 5, 1962, a great screen legend died of a drug overdose in the bedroom of her small home in Los Angeles's Brentwood section. Nude, sprawled across her bed, clutching her telephone, Marilyn Monroe was discovered by her housekeeper, Eunice Murray. Sometime after 5 A.M. Marilyn's body was removed to Crypt 33 at the L.A. County Morgue and assigned coroner's case no. 81128. When the news broke, friends and fans reeled in shock and sorrow. The whole world mourned. It seemed impossible that the quintessential movie star and sex symbol was gone at the age of thirty-six.

But who *was* Marilyn Monroe? Who was the woman behind the glitter, the glamour, and the rumors? The answer is complicated: She was a dreamer who lived in a nightmare. She was part myth, part media creation, and part orphan. She was driven and ambitious but weak and vulnerable; she was charismatic and magnetic but emotionally unstable and even paranoid. By the end of her days she was what she had always aspired to be—a serious actress—yet was also what she had always dreaded being—an unstable woman whose personal life and career were in shambles.

Marilyn Monroe remains alive in the

hearts of generations of fans. We laugh at her comedic performances, marvel at her dramatic roles, and pity her for the tragic elements of her life and her loss, so early, of what she defined as a star's "right to twinkle."

It would have comforted her to know that, three decades later, she shines brightly on.

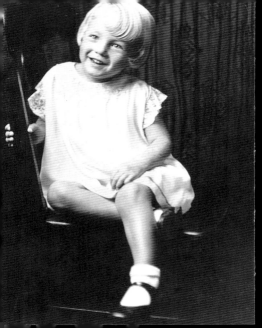

THE EARLY YEARS
(1926–44)

THE CHILD WHO would one day become Marilyn Monroe was named Norma Jean Mortensen when she was born in Los Angeles on June 1, 1926. Her mother, Gladys, a film cutter, was separated but not yet divorced from her second husband, Martin Mortensen, and Norma Jean was, in fact, illegitimate; her father was C. Stanley Gifford, with whom Gladys worked at RKO studios.

Neither Gifford nor Gladys's mother, Della Monroe, provided Gladys with any emotional or financial support, so Norma

Jean was soon placed in the first of several foster homes. She was a child born into a maternal legacy of severe mental illness. Her great-grandfather had committed suicide; both her grandfather, Otis, and her grandmother were institutionalized at the time of their deaths; and her mother was committed to a mental hospital when Norma Jean was only seven. Except for a few brief interludes, Gladys was institutionalized until and beyond the death of her famous daughter, Marilyn Monroe.

Norma Jean was shuffled from guardians to foster families until the age of nine when her mother's friend Grace McKee finally placed her in the Los Angeles Orphan's Home. She lived there for two years until Grace, who had married in the interim, reclaimed her. Grace put the girl with two other families before finally bringing Norma Jean into her own home. In her autobiography many years later, Marilyn described Grace as "the first person who ever patted my head or touched my cheek." She added: "I can still remember how thrilled I felt when her kind hand touched me."

The absence of a loving family and a stable home environment scarred Norma Jean for life. As an adult, she attempted to create several substitute families, but nothing diminished the feelings of abandonment and loneliness that remained etched into the core of her personality.

"This sad, bitter child who grew up too fast is hardly ever out of my heart," she later wrote. "With success all around me, I can still feel her frightened eyes looking out of mine. She keeps saying, 'I never lived, I was never loved,' and often I get confused and think it's I who am saying it."

Norma Jean attended Emerson Junior High School and Van Nuys High School. In her free time, she learned the tenets of Christian Science from Grace's aunt, Ana Lower, whom Norma Jean loved and remained close to until the woman's death in 1948.

As a child, Norma Jean was thrilled by the movies and reenacted dramatic scenes behind the closed door of her bedroom. She also developed a deep desire to be beautiful, so beautiful, in her own words, "that people would turn around on the street to stare at her."

She matured early, and just eleven days after her sixteenth birthday—probably due to Grace's manipulations and certainly with her blessings—Norma Jean married Jim Dougherty, a twenty-one-year-old neighbor who worked for Lockheed Aircraft. Norma Jean immediately dropped out of high school to be a full-time wife and homemaker; from all reports, she and Jim were happy until he joined the merchant marines and shipped out two years later. Norma Jean begged him to stay and viewed his leaving as another terrible abandonment.

With her husband away for a year at a stretch, Norma Jean became lonely and bored. Eventually she sought the company of other men, sometimes exchanging sex for spending money. Finally, she joined the war effort and went to work alongside her mother-in-law at Radio Plane in Van Nuys. Starting as a parachute packer, she was soon shifted to the department where the plane fuselages were sprayed with liquid plastic. She worked hard and earned an "E for Excellent" in her employee evaluation after only a few months on the job.

All the changes that later occurred in Norma Jean's life can be traced directly to that job at Radio Plane: that's where she was discovered by army photographer David Conover, who was assigned to take publicity shots of women working to support the war effort. Because of those photographs, Norma Jean's life as an average person ended and her life as a model, a beauty, and a sex symbol began.

"I knew I belonged to the public and to the world, not because I was talented or even beautiful but because I had never belonged to anything or anyone else."

THE DREAM BEGINS
(1944–50)

ARMED WITH THE pictures Conover took, Norma Jean approached Emmeline Snively, the head of the Blue Book Models School. Miss Snively saw her enormous potential and immediately arranged to have Norma Jean trained and sent on assignments.

Success as a model came quickly, so she was soon one of the most popular cover girls in California. Luxuriating in the "star treatment," she quite naturally began to think of the glamour of Hollywood. As a child, in the brief period before her mother was institutionalized, the movies had been a crucial part of Norma Jean's picture of a happy life. Now she wanted to *be* a part of that magical world.

Unfortunately, at the same time she was achieving notoriety as a model, she suffered from bouts of depression—a foreshadowing of her later years. In fact, she admitted to two suicide attempts by age nineteen.

Norma Jean spent her twentieth birthday in Las Vegas, waiting out the six weeks' residency requirement for a divorce from Jim Dougherty. The divorce was as much a career move as a personal one. She had learned that the Hollywood studios usually rejected married women as possible starlets. And Norma Jean intended, in no uncertain terms, to be a starlet.

At Emmeline Snively's prodding, Norma Jean bleached her dark blonde hair to a much lighter, brighter shade and moved into the Studio Club, a quasi boarding house for young women trying to break into the movies. In July 1946, she made an unscheduled call on Ben Lyon, the head of new talent at Twentieth Century-Fox, and walked away with her first contract. Describing her as "absolutely gorgeous," Lyon arranged a screen test in which she sizzled while doing nothing more than lighting a cigarette and crossing a room. He hired her at the going rate of seventy-five dollars per week.

However, he wasn't happy with her name. She had used many variations, including Norma Jean Baker (her mother's first husband's surname) and Jean Norman, but Lyon suggested Marilyn. Norma Jean added her grandmother's last name—Monroe.

On that day, in that office, Marilyn Monroe was born. Except in her most intimate relationships, Norma Jean faded away and Marilyn Monroe, the sexy screen goddess, emerged and reigned till the end of her days.

Suddenly one of more than three dozen contract players, Marilyn immersed herself in singing, dancing, and acting lessons. She first landed a tiny part in a movie called *Scudda Hoo! Scudda Hay!* Most of her on-screen time was cut, but Marilyn said she didn't mind. "I knew I would be better in the next picture," she commented. This was followed by a bit part in *Dangerous Years*, but the studio executives were unimpressed and terminated her contract after the first year.

Marilyn Monroe was unemployed and desperate, but in March her sometime-lover Joe Schenck, an executive producer and cofounder of Twentieth Century-Fox, arranged an interview at Columbia Pictures; soon she was under contract again.

During her entire early career, powerful men—and sometimes women—were smitten by this beautiful blonde with the breathy baby voice and the aura of innocence and vulnerability. Many helped her. But superagent Johnny Hyde is universally credited with carving out Marilyn's big breaks and transforming her into a household name.

Hyde wined, dined, dressed, and introduced her to the starmakers of Hollywood. He was also hopelessly in love with her. He divorced his wife and begged Marilyn to marry him, swearing to leave her millions when he died—which, he dryly promised, would be shortly. But Marilyn refused. Though she was his devoted live-in mistress, she revealed to several friends (and also in her 1974 autobiography, *My Story*) that she felt marrying Johnny Hyde without loving him would be dishonest and unfair. "What have you got to lose?" her exasperated ex-lover, Joe Schenck, demanded. "Myself," Marilyn answered.

Marilyn's notoriety soared when she appeared in the Marx Brothers' *Love Happy*. The role called for her to walk, in the words of Groucho Marx, "in such a manner as to arouse my elderly libido and cause smoke to issue from my ears." When Marilyn did as directed, she got the job. "And don't do any walking in unpoliced areas," Harpo advised. *Love Happy* and the publicity tour that followed greatly enhanced Marilyn's siren image, though the role that changed the shape and direction of her career came to her due to an odd set of typically Hollywood circumstances.

It was 1949, and John Huston was casting a crime drama called *The Asphalt Jungle*. A great director known for his extravagant taste and subsequent chronic cash-flow problems, Huston was at the time eighteen thousand dollars in hock for the room and board of his twenty-three racehorses. The woman to whom he owed the money, Lucille Ryman, an old friend of Marilyn's, threatened to attach Huston's salary unless he tested Marilyn for the role of a gangster's "niece."

After the screen test Huston gave the

part to Marilyn with no reservations: she was perfect for it. Johnny Hyde negotiated her salary up to $350 per week. Shortly afterward, he upped that to $500 per week for the duration of Marilyn's next picture, the Bette Davis vehicle *All About Eve.* Hyde also convinced Darryl Zanuck, who had originally snubbed Marilyn, to sign her to a long-term contract at Twentieth Century-Fox.

Marilyn Monroe, the blonde bombshell who measured 35-22-35 and walked with a provocative wiggle—largely because she cut a quarter-inch off one of her heels to ensure that effect—was now firmly on the road to superstardom. She was not quite twenty-five years old.

"I'm a failure as a woman. My men expect so much of me, because of the image they've made of me and that I've made of myself, as a sex symbol. Men expect so much, and I can't live up to it. They expect bells to ring and whistles to whistle, but my anatomy is the same as any other woman's. I can't live up to it."

THE DREAM COMES TRUE
(1950–55)

MARILYN MONROE WON critical acclaim for *The Asphalt Jungle* and *All About Eve*, and her life appeared to be a storybook success story—but then tragedy struck. Johnny Hyde died of a heart attack on December 16, 1950. Two days later, despite his deathbed request that "Marilyn be treated as one of the family," his family threw her out of his house. Soon after, while staying with her acting coach and friend Natasha Lytess, Marilyn attempted suicide by drug overdose. Natasha found her just in time.

Her emotional recovery was slow even as her career moved along the fast star track. As film after film was released—six in 1950 alone—Marilyn was viewed as a hot property by any standard. She basked in the adulation and attention, but she desperately wanted to be a fine actress, too, not merely a sex symbol.

She enrolled in acting classes conducted by Michael Chekhov, nephew of the great Russian playwright Anton Chekhov. Painfully insecure about her ability and artistry, she began to acquire a reputation for late arrivals on the set and an inability to remember lines. Yet world-class directors—like John Huston and Fritz Lang, who directed her in *Clash by Night*—raved about her on-screen luminosity and her raw talent.

In the midst of it all, scandal broke. Marilyn Monroe was identified as the subject of a nude photo used for a calendar. Studio heads huddled and planned press releases, yet Marilyn defied them all and simply told the truth: she had posed for the calendar for fifty dollars in her modeling days when she was broke and desperate. As the movie executives held their collective breath, the public, completely enamored with Marilyn, forgave her. Her popularity remained undiminished.

Soon afterward, nosy reporters learned that her mother was not dead, as Marilyn had claimed. Marilyn then admitted that

Gladys was institutionalized, and the second scandal blew over.

During her rise to fame, Marilyn had many affairs. But when she met ex-Yankee outfielder Joe DiMaggio, their sexual chemistry soon ignited into full-blown love. The world watched with awe as the sports hero courted the screen goddess whose popularity continued to rise. Audiences applauded her performances in five films in 1952 and three in 1953—including a thriller, *Niagara*, with Joseph Cotten; a musical comedy, *Gentlemen Prefer Blondes*, with Jane Russell; and a comedy, *How to Marry a Millionaire*, with Betty Grable and Lauren Bacall. In 1953, she won *Photoplay* magazine's Gold Star

Award for the fastest-rising new star, and fan letters poured in at the rate of five thousand per week.

DiMaggio and Monroe married on January 14, 1954, but the marriage was destined to last only nine months. DiMaggio's possessiveness, discomfort with his wife's role as every man's dream woman, and pressure on Marilyn to put her career aside for him took too heavy a toll, so their marriage came to a painful and public end on the grounds of mental cruelty and "conflict of careers."

Despite Marilyn's frequent statements about her strong desire to be a wife—and particularly a mother—she always found marriage confining and problematic. She also had several abortions and tragically miscarried the only two babies she felt able to have and keep.

By 1955, Marilyn was also suffering from the effects of too much alcohol and too many drugs. A chronic insomniac, she had long used barbiturates. This, in part, can be blamed on the studio executives, who encouraged doctors to prescribe pills to keep their stars functional. Prescription drug use in the mid-1950s was rampant, and Marilyn Monroe was certainly no exception.

After the demise of her second marriage and in the midst of better and better film reviews, Marilyn grew increasingly discontent. She was trapped in the "dumb blonde" sex-symbol persona and bound by an outdated and unfair contract.

She disappeared for ten days in December 1954, then flew to New York to live with Milton and Amy Greene. Milton was a photographer who had worked with Marilyn two years before and convinced her to take control of her career. Marilyn announced their business partnership on January 1, 1955. In one fell swoop, Marilyn Monroe turned her back on Hollywood and became the president of her own production company—Marilyn Monroe Productions.

"The truth is I've never fooled anyone. I've let men sometimes fool themselves. Men sometimes didn't bother to find out who and what I was. Instead they would invent a character for me. I wouldn't argue with them."

THE NEW MARILYN EMERGES
(1955–60)

WITH MILTON GREENE supplying career guidance and money, and Marilyn supplying not only talent but also the hottest screen property—herself—in the world, success seemed inevitable. Greene negotiated with Fox a new contract that promised Marilyn one hundred thousand dollars minimum per picture, script approval, and freedom to work for other studios. This was a major and much-discussed coup for the "dumb blonde."

Under the careful support of the

Greenes, Marilyn slowly reinvented herself. She enrolled in private study with Lee Strasberg, founder of the famed Actor's Studio. Lee and his wife, Paula, remained critically important to Marilyn for the rest of her life. Lee was her trusted mentor and friend; in fact, she left him the bulk of her personal estate when she died. And Paula became her private acting coach, never leaving Marilyn's side (unless she was barred from the set, which happened periodically) until her last picture.

Since Lee Strasberg's "method" acting involved intensive probing of one's past and a great deal of soul searching, he encouraged Marilyn (and all his students) to undergo psychotherapy. Marilyn began analysis with a psychiatrist named Dr. Marianne Kris.

As Milton Greene secured the rights to a Broadway play that would become Marilyn's next picture, Marilyn immersed herself in study at the Actor's Studio. Given no special treatment there, she worked on her craft and herself. And she fell in love with playwright Arthur Miller, whom she had met for the first time just after Johnny Hyde's death. Meeting in secret for nearly a year until Miller's divorce was finalized, they were finally married in private on June 29, 1956. Two weeks later they flew to England, where Marilyn began work on Marilyn Monroe Productions' first independent feature:

The Prince and the Showgirl, which costarred and was directed by Laurence Olivier.

On the surface, Marilyn was on top of the world: married to a highly respected writer and intellectual, with opportunities and power that most actresses could never dare to dream of. But under this facade little Norma Jean—the abandoned, unloved, and insecure child—was demanding more and more from Marilyn Monroe, the phenomenon she had created as a cover-up.

Marilyn was terrified of acting with Laurence Olivier (considered by many to be the greatest living actor) and horrified by Olivier's "harsh" directing style, which was so opposite to the Strasberg "method" she trusted. She desired challenging acting roles yet felt deeply inadequate. Unable to cope with this constant inner torment, she turned more and more to pills and alcohol for relief. Arthur Miller, just two months into their marriage, became Marilyn's nursemaid and baby-sitter, carefully monitoring her pill intake and pushing her to the movie set.

Marilyn's repeated tardiness looks somewhat different, however, when viewed as an avoidance tactic. Marilyn had fought her way to the big leagues, where the stakes were highest, only to discover that her own unmanageable internal pressures were crushing her. Her New York psychiatrist, Dr. Kris, was flown to England to help stabilize her.

Still, intense animosity developed on the picture, smoothed over only by Milton Greene. The Miller/Monroe marriage appeared to be in trouble too. It recovered, but Marilyn's relationship with Milton Greene, whom she viewed as a traitor for sometimes siding with Olivier, didn't. Their partnership, so important to Marilyn's independence and personal growth, dissolved after only one picture.

Back in the States, Marilyn and Arthur Miller settled into a troubled marriage. There were tentatively happy times and seriously tragic ones. Marilyn miscarried two babies. She made a second serious suicide attempt. Miller saved her at least twice from unintentional overdoses. And while her movie performances were consistently praised, her behind-the-scenes behavior was, by industry standards, deplorable. On the set of *Some Like It Hot*, she routinely showed up several hours late for her calls. She couldn't remember dialogue—in fact, she required as many as sixty takes to get one usable sentence. And she suffered several "collapses" on the set. Studio heads began to watch her with skepticism.

With the great Arthur Miller reduced to the role of caretaker, their marriage began to unravel. Marilyn started a love affair with Yves Montand, who was her costar in *Let's Make Love*, and was married to actress Simone Signoret. Their affair was public knowledge. Between her pills and alcohol, kamikaze career moves, and marriage troubles, Marilyn Monroe was locked in a downward spiral that inexorably moved her toward disaster.

"I am not interested in money.
I just want to be wonderful."

THE FINAL ACT: THE END OF
THE LEGEND
(1960–62)

AT THE END of her marriage, Marilyn
starred in *The Misfits*, which Arthur Miller
wrote especially for her. It was the last film
she would ever complete. A sensitive, art-
ful film directed by John Huston, it told
the story of an isolated, lonely woman who
befriends three troubled cowboys while
waiting in Reno for her divorce.

It starred Clark Gable, whom young
Norma Jean had often fantasized was her

father, Montgomery Clift, and Eli
Wallach. From the start, the production
was disastrous. Since the character she
played was so much like herself, she found
the role extremely difficult. Temperatures
hovered at one hundred degrees, and
Marilyn kept the entire cast waiting for
hours while she attempted to compose
herself. Her director felt she was taking as
many as twenty sleeping pills a day, and
rumors flew that she had come near death
and had had her stomach pumped. She
was removed from the set and taken to
Los Angeles to be placed in the care of
her California psychiatrist, Dr. Ralph
Greenson.

She returned later, and the film stumbled

toward completion. When it finally wrapped, Marilyn and Arthur Miller announced their plans for divorce. Their marriage had lasted four years.

The Misfits opened to some harsh reviews, and, severely distraught, Marilyn entered New York's Paine Whitney Psychiatric Clinic. Even more desperate once inside, she turned to ex-husband Joe DiMaggio to get her out, and he transferred her to Columbia Presbyterian Medical Center so she could withdraw from her pill dependency. Their friendship, raised from the ashes of her marriage to Miller, lasted until her death.

The last few years of Marilyn Monroe's life were a sad testimony of worsening pill addiction and encroaching mental illness. Even though she had a solid support system, including Dr. Greenson and the Strasbergs, Marilyn was losing control. She saw her psychiatrist sometimes seven days a week, and became a beloved member of Dr. Greenson's extended family. She even made steps toward stabilizing herself by buying her first home, a modest one-story house with a small kidney-shaped pool.

However, she didn't work in 1961, and when the studio forced her to honor the final picture of her Fox contract by appearing in the prophetically named *Something's Got to Give*, her total lack of cooperation—she showed up for work only one out of every three days—ultimately got her fired and sued for half a million dollars. Marilyn certainly thought she would be rehired but instead she was replaced. The era of Marilyn Monroe the movie star was over.

It was during this last phase of her life, after a quick divorce from Arthur Miller, that Marilyn had affairs with singer Frank Sinatra; the attorney general, Robert F. Kennedy; and the president of the United States, John F. Kennedy. Much has been made of her affair with JFK, which may have begun as early as 1955, and of her famous rendition of "Happy Birthday" at the Madison Square Garden rally for Kennedy's birthday on May 19, 1962. Her numerous rendezvous with the president at New York's Carlyle Hotel are a matter of record.

Yet the deeper love she felt for Kennedy's younger brother, Robert, is often underrated. In her delusionary state, she fantasized that RFK, a Roman Catholic, would leave his wife and family and marry her. And though it was not reported at the time, rumors have persisted to this day that RFK visited Marilyn on the final afternoon of her life, probably to break off their relationship.

The reasons for this break are complicated. Through Sinatra, Marilyn was casually connected with certain Mafia figures, like Sam Giancana, against whom RFK had launched a serious legal campaign.

As attorney general of the United States, RFK could not afford to associate with her. Also, her behavior was becoming too erratic and dangerous for him; according to some accounts, she threatened to hold a press conference to reveal their affair.

But no one really knows what happened on the night of August 4. Was her overdose unintentional as so many others had been? Or did Marilyn Monroe take her own life? Or, as many people assert, was she murdered?

We do know that, by the end, she had retreated into a fantasy world in which her moods swung from mistrust and paranoia to grandiose expectations of marrying into a political dynasty. We know her

psychological, alcohol, and drug problems
had escalated to the point where she was
completely unable to cope. After all,
though we tend to forget it, Marilyn
Monroe was only human. Her
autopsy report describes her
simply as a "well-nourished
Caucasian female, weighing
117 pounds and measuring
65 1/2 inches in length."

"To put it bluntly, I seem to have a whole superstructure with no foundation. But I'm working on the foundation."

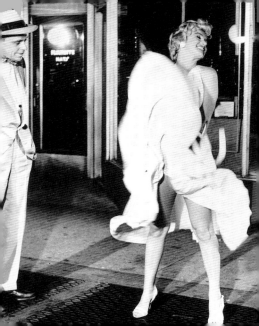

AFTERWORD

HOW SHOULD MARILYN Monroe be remembered? As an isolated, fearful orphan who desperately needed love and approval? As Hollywood's idea of the perfect woman, who embodied both raw sex appeal and childlike innocence? As a stunningly beautiful starlet who rose to glory only to self-destruct?

Marilyn would probably want to be remembered as a woman who worked hard to fulfill her dream. She sought to be more than she was at any given moment: more than a factory worker, more than a model, more than a sex symbol. For all her weaknesses, there was a core of strength in her that demanded she seek and find her true identity as both a person and an actress. And she would probably want to be remembered for the pleasure she has brought and continues to bring her fans.

Despite her tragic end, she remains a beloved icon in the history of movie-making. She was a complex individual and a true original—one of a kind.

"In Hollywood a girl's virtue is much less important than her hairdo. . . . Hollywood's a place where they'll pay you a thousand dollars for a kiss, and fifty cents for your soul. I know, because I turned down the first offer often enough and held out for the fifty cents."

FILMOGRAPHY

(dates are release dates):

1947 **DANGEROUS YEARS**
TWENTIETH CENTURY-FOX
Director: Arthur Pierson

1948 **SCUDDA HOO! SCUDDA HAY!**
(her first film but second release)
TWENTIETH CENTURY-FOX
Director: F. Hugh Herbert

1948 **LADIES OF THE CHORUS**
COLUMBIA PICTURES
Director: Phil Karlson

1950 **LOVE HAPPY**

UNITED ARTISTS

Director: David Miller

1950 **A TICKET TO TOMAHAWK**

TWENTIETH CENTURY-FOX

Director: Richard Sale

1950 **THE ASPHALT JUNGLE**

METRO-GOLDWYN-MAYER

Director: John Huston

1950 **ALL ABOUT EVE**

TWENTIETH CENTURY-FOX

Director: Joseph L. Mankiewicz

1950 **THE FIREBALL**

TWENTIETH CENTURY-FOX

Director: Tay Garnett

1950 RIGHT CROSS

METRO-GOLDWYN-MAYER

Director: John Sturges

1951 HOMETOWN STORY

METRO-GOLDWYN-MAYER

Director: Arthur Pierson

1951 AS YOUNG AS YOU FEEL

TWENTIETH CENTURY-FOX

Director: Harmon Jones

1951 LOVE NEST

TWENTIETH CENTURY-FOX

Director: Joseph Newman

1951 LET'S MAKE IT LEGAL

TWENTIETH CENTURY-FOX

Director: Richard Sale

1952 CLASH BY NIGHT

RKO RADIO

Director: Fritz Lang

1952 WE'RE NOT MARRIED

TWENTIETH CENTURY-FOX

Director: Edmund Goulding

1952 DON'T BOTHER TO KNOCK

TWENTIETH CENTURY-FOX

Director: Roy Baker

1952 MONKEY BUSINESS

TWENTIETH CENTURY-FOX

Director: Howard Hawks

1952 O. HENRY'S FULL HOUSE

TWENTIETH CENTURY-FOX

Director: Henry Hathaway

1953 NIAGARA

TWENTIETH CENTURY-FOX

Director: Henry Hathaway

1953 GENTLEMEN PREFER BLONDES

TWENTIETH CENTURY-FOX

Director: Howard Hawks

1953 HOW TO MARRY A MILLIONAIRE

TWENTIETH CENTURY-FOX

Director: Jean Negulesco

1954 RIVER OF NO RETURN

TWENTIETH CENTURY-FOX

Director: Otto Preminger

1954 THERE'S NO BUSINESS LIKE SHOW BUSINESS

TWENTIETH CENTURY-FOX

Director: Walter Lang

1955 THE SEVEN YEAR ITCH

TWENTIETH CENTURY-FOX

Director: Billy Wilder

1956 BUS STOP

TWENTIETH CENTURY-FOX

Director: Joshua Logan

1957 THE PRINCE AND THE SHOWGIRL

WARNER BROTHERS

Director: Laurence Olivier

1959 SOME LIKE IT HOT

UNITED ARTISTS

Director: Billy Wilder

1960 LET'S MAKE LOVE

TWENTIETH CENTURY-FOX

Director: George Cukor

1961 THE MISFITS

UNITED ARTISTS

Director: John Huston

The text of this book was set in Electra, and
the display was set in Futura Light, by
Snap-Haus Graphics, Dumont, New Jersey.

Book Design by
Diane Stevenson / Snap-Haus Graphics